# EMPTY BEACHES

## POEMS BY BRETT FLEISHMAN
### ILLUSTRATIONS BY SAM WHITE

Published by Mindstir Media LLC

45 Lafayette Rd. Suite 181 | North Hampton, NH 03862 | USA

1.800.767.0531 | www.mindstirmedia.com

Printed in the United States of America

ISBN-13: 978-0-9993872-1-4

Library of Congress Control Number: 2017913717

MINDSTIR MEDIA

This book is dedicated to Jacob...
No one has shown more excitement
for my writing than you have.
Thanks for being so supportive!

"Always dream big.
It's OK if you do.
If you don't there's no way
That your dream will come true."

# WORDPLAYS

I love using wordplays in my poems. My favorite wordplays are puns and idioms. If you don't know what puns and idioms are, that's OK. I define them in the appendix of this book. I also explain, poem by poem, what makes these puns and idioms funny (well, funny to me, that is).

How will you know whether the poem has a pun or an idiom in it? Great question!

If you see (P) at the end of the poem, it means there is a pun at the end of the poem. If you see (I) at the end of the poem, it means there is an idiom at the end of the poem. If you don't see either, it means the poem doesn't have a pun or an idiom in it.

Got it? Good! Come on in…

# TABLE OF CONTENTS

# WEIGHTLIFTING CONTEST

As they sit at a bar by the edge of a pool
Two enormous weightlifters each sit on a stool

The first weightlifter brags, 'I'm much stronger than you!'
The next weightlifter claims, 'There's no way that is true!'

So, to prove he is right, the first weightlifter stands
Then he pulls his stool out of the ground with bare hands

The next weightlifter stands. Briefly he looks around.
With one heave he dislodges two stools from the ground

The first weightlifter can't believe he's been outdone
He is losing this contest. This isn't much fun.

Well aware he is losing, which isn't the goal
The first weightlifter spots near the ground a large hole

The hole's under the stools of the bar, near the base
When he sees this a smile appears on his face

He kneels near the large hole, with both hands holds on tight
He then hoists himself up, does with all of his might .

Using powerful force and before he once blinks
The first weightlifter lifts the bar counter and drinks

The next weightlifter watches in awe from afar
There's no doubt the first weightlifter just raised the bar [1]

# WORLD TRAVELERS?

'It's time to plan our next class trip'
The teacher tells her students
'But there's not much cash.
So, as you're planning, use some prudence!'

'I've a perfect place to go.
How long's the flight to Delhi?'
Someone asks the teacher
(I believe that it was Nelly)

'We have got an awesome place.
Can we head to Brazil?'
Ask three kids in unison
(They're Jill and Bill and Will)

'I love eating.
Can we take a trip to visit Florence?'
Says a boy who's never been
(A hungry boy named Lawrence)

'I prefer a different spot.
Can we please see Grenada?'
Asks the shyest girl in class
(This girl's name is Renata)

'If we only take one trip
We must head to Geneva'
Vows the most demanding girl
(So self-assured is Riva)

'One place I have never been
But want to go is Greece.
If we take a trip
I'd love to head there!', states Denise

Now the final student speaks
With confidence does Harris
'If we're going anywhere
It really should be Paris!'

None too pleased, the teacher sighs
She slowly shakes her head
'These trips are expensive!
Did you not hear what I said?'

'Our trip's off.  Forget it!'
She yells at the stunned classmates
Unaware these places
Were in the United States

If you ever take a U.S. road trip...
Be sure to check out these places:

*Delhi, California*
*Brazil, Indiana*
*Florence, South Carolina*
*Grenada, Mississippi*
*Geneva, Illinois*
*Greece, New York*
*Paris, Texas*

# SCHOOL BUS FACTORY TOUR

They make school buses here, six or seven a day
The mechanics who build them are skilled I must say

They are so skilled, in fact, every bus comes out right
They give factory tours that are truly a sight

The next tour has been scheduled for late afternoon
It is now 4 o'clock.  The tour's gonna start soon.

The proud boss introduces himself to the crowd
'Please feel free to take pictures.  Your phones are allowed.'

The boss starts in a room where the tires get made
'We use only fine rubber.  It must be high-grade.'

They next visit a room where they make steering wheels
'They're the safest around!', the boss proudly reveals

As they head down the hall, a mechanic walks by
'This is Russ,' the boss says.  'He's a heckuva guy!'

They continue the tour, check out several more rooms
After one bathroom break, the school bus tour resumes

In the next-to-last room, they are making the seats
'They're so comfy, so comfy!', the proud boss repeats

As they exit this room, they head to the last one
The boss says, 'Let's check out a school bus once it's done!'

In this room there's one shiny school bus on the floor
Russ tells them to come in.  'Don't just stand by the door!'

As the crowd gathers 'round the school bus they can see
Under it oil leaks.  Oh, no!  How can that be?

As the boss glares at Russ, horrified by the scene
He becomes quite upset and, to Russ, he acts mean

'This is clearly your fault!  There should not be a leak!'
Russ would like to respond.  The boss won't let him speak.

Moments later the boss shoves Russ hard to the ground
Russ falls backwards and trips, then he spins twice around

Russ slows down and, at last, he is finally still
With his body now drenched in the huge oil spill

The crowd feels really bad that this happened to Russ
Why the heck would his boss throw him under the bus? [1]

# CHECK, PRETTY PLEASE?

For five hours two kings have enjoyed tasty meals
They've shared lobster and steak.  One king even tried eels!

Half past midnight their waiter is starting to grieve
He's exhausted and desperately wanting to leave

Though he must be polite (these are kings after all!)
This poor waiter knows if they don't leave he'll soon bawl

After thinking of ways he can drop subtle hints
He brings out a small tray filled with end-of-meal mints

The two kings thank the waiter, continue to chat
They did not get his hint...oh well, so much for that!

Though the waiter's frustrated, he stays quite composed
He says gently, 'Please note that our kitchen just closed'

The kings thank him, so kindly, for sharing the news
As the waiter steps out, they continue to schmooze

When the waiter returns, he is clutching their bill
*I must be more direct with these kings.  Yes, I will!*

After taking a breath, he with confidence states
'I am leaving real soon, so I'll get your check mates' [P]

# STOP SIGN FIASCO

There are 35 stops signs lined up on one road
And, to no one's surprise, now the traffic has slowed

The cars aren't moving slowly.  They've screeched to a halt.
All the cops hear complaints, but it's not the cops' fault

Since the cops cannot take this complaining much more
They come up with a deal that's too good to ignore

The cops tell all the drivers, 'If you do not whine
We will quickly remove every single stop sign'

Though they like the cops' plan (it has lots of appeal)
The mad drivers insist the cops sweeten the deal

'We'll agree to your deal.  We'll agree right away.
But you must remove 35 stop signs today'

The cops don't think the terms of this deal are quite fair
Yet they quickly agree.  'We will pull them.  We swear!'

For the next seven hours, the cops try their best
They don't take any breaks.  There is no time to rest.

They've pulled 25 signs.  The sun's starting to set.
But the cops do not quit with 10 signs to pull yet

They pull stop signs alone.  They pull stop signs together.
They pull some stop signs in pretty bad weather

It's nearly 12.  Yes, it's almost midnight.
There's one stop sign still standing, far off to the right

The cops fall to their knees.  They can now barely move.
They crawl up to the last sign they've yet to remove

With one minute to go, the cops pull the sign out
'Yes, we did it!', the cops do excitedly shout

They accomplished their goal, did these hardworking cops
They succeeded because they pulled out all the stops [1]

# RODEO RICK

He was raised in Wyoming was Rodeo Rick
The best cowboy around, he could do any trick

He could lasso a calf from a mile away
He could hurdle his horse over 10 stacks of hay

But one day something happened, so sad, on his horse
The horse saw a small mouse, then jumped back with great force

And the force of this jump knocked Rick down to the ground
Where he lay in great pain with nobody around

After 25 minutes, Rick angrily cried
'I am done with these horses!  No more shall I ride!'

For the next 15 years, Rick did honor his vow
(This brings you up to speed.  Rick is 25 now.)

Though he no longer rides, Rick loves rodeo shows
When a great rider rides, Rick nostalgically glows

So tonight, at the rodeo, Rick is impressed
When a beautiful cowgirl is voted the best

At the end of the night, Rick seeks out this fine gal
(Did I mention her name?  Her name's Rodeo Val.)

Rick tells Val she was great.  'Watching you was a joy.
It brought back memories of when I was a boy.'

He tells Val 'bout his past, of the day he fell down
'I have not ridden since,' Rick tells Val with a frown

Val tells Rick, 'Your fall happened a decade ago.
Try once more.  You might like it.  You just never know.'

After thinking this through, Rick tells Val he sure will
Then Val says, 'Let's go now!  It will be a big thrill!'

Rick responds, 'Sure, why not!', but Val sees Rick looks tense
She says, 'Let's ride those horses beside the white fence!'

Once they reach the two horses, Val jumps aboard first
She does not hesitate.  Val hops up with a burst.

Rick looks up knowing this is his moment to seize
Then he hoists himself onto the saddle with ease

Rick is back on a horse, first time since he was 10
He looks happy.  Rick's back in the saddle again. [I]

# MR. EXAGGERATION

My Dad says I'm so, so, so, so, SO, so melancholic
Am I really sad or is Dad way too hyperbolic?

# ZANY WORD BLENDER #1
## (boy names)

There's a mouse who keeps stealing my cheese     _____

It is furry and scampers with ease     _____

Though I keep a trap out     _____

This sly mouse angles out     _____

I may need a new mousetrap soon, jeez     _____

*Inside each line, I hid one word*

*Combine them since, right now, they're blurred*

# DICTIONARY

This dictionary's fun to read. I will not take a break.
I should be done by 10 PM if I can stay awake
*(Tiny yawn)*

The first word in my book's *aardvark*. *A-a* words are unique.
My favorite *B's bedazzled*. In the *C's*, I like *critique*.
*(Small yawn)*

The *D* words seem so tedious. I don't like *dull* and *dreary*.
The *E* words look inviting even though one word is *eerie*
*(Bigger yawn)*

Though I am feeling sleepy now, my goal's to make it through
There are so many cool words starting with the letter *Q*
*(Big yawn)*

Some *F* words I have never seen, like *feign* and *finicky*
Most *G* words I have memorized, except for *gimmicky*
*(Gigantic yawn)*

One *H* word looks so strange to me. *Herl* won't throw me off track!
I'm halfway through the *I* words. What's this one: *insomniac?*
*(Snore)*

# LOTTERY TICKET

'Buy a lottery ticket.  Today's the big day!'
The convenience store owner encourages Jay

After learning the jackpot is 12 million bucks
Jay buys one ticket, then out the door the boy ducks

He runs back to his house, doesn't want to be late
They'll announce the big winner sometime around eight

In his kitchen, back home, Jay turns on his T.V.
On his ticket are 6, 8, 1, 2, 5 and 3

Jay puts his ticket down near the large kitchen sink
*I am going to win!*, Jay's beginning to think

On the T.V. a man says, 'It's time for the picks!'
Then he reads the first number.  The pick is a 6.

Jay's excited, of course.  Things are starting off great.
The man reads the next number.  Good news!  It's an 8!

What an excellent start!  Jay is having such fun.
Soon he hears the next number.  No way!  It's a 1!

Jay has matched all three numbers.  He's now halfway through.
Then he hears the man say, 'The next pick is a 2!'

Jay is nervous but pleased.  Somehow he's still alive.
The man proudly declares, 'The next pick is a 5!'

Jay has nailed all five picks!  Truly, how can this be?
He'll win 12 million bucks if the last pick is 3!

It's a very big moment, this Jay understands
Feeling sweaty he pours water onto his hands

As he lifts up his hands, wiping his sweaty head
By mistake Jay bumps into his ticket instead

It falls into the sink with the water still on
He must grab it, right now, or else it will be gone!

As Jay reaches his hand in the sink very quick
The man on T.V. says, 'It's a 3, the last pick!'

Jay has just won the lottery if he can save
His wet ticket that's sinking, the outlook is grave

Soon his ticket is gone.  This is truly insane.
Poor Jay's ticket and hopes have both gone down the drain [1]

# TUG-OF-WAR

On this piping hot coal, brave foods play Tug-of-War
Both the steaks and the fish have squared off here before

But whenever they battle, the fish seem to win
They tug harder and faster each time they begin

So, before the next war, Captain Steak tells his team
'If we tug harder first, they will run out of steam'

The steaks heed his advice.  They tug hard from the start.
The fish don't take the lead, so the Captain looks smart

But the fish do not quit.  They're as strong as the steaks.
They do not want to lose.  They will do what it takes.

As the war carries on, the hot coals burn the feet
Of the steaks and the fish who tip-toe in the heat

Captain Steak, so excited, yells out a decree
'Tug as hard as you can once I count down from three!'

Once the Captain counts down, the steaks tug super hard
Now the fish drop the rope, which is totally charred

Captain Steak tells his team, 'Yes, we did it!  We won!
I am proud of you steaks.  This was very well done!' (P)

# POTATO CHIP WAR

A 12-year-old boy
And his six-year-old brother
Chomp some potato chips
Next to their mother

When the tween asks
'Can you please pass the chips?'
As the six-year-old does
He mistakenly trips

The bag falls to the ground
Chips fly out everywhere
On the 12-year-old's shirt
On his shoes, in his hair

When the six-year-old laughs
His big brother does roar
'I do hereby declare
A Potato Chip War!'

As he says this he scopes
Where the six-year-old stands
Then he hurls some chips at him
With both of his hands

Since the six-year-old boy
Can't escape this attack
The chips land on his legs
On his feet, on his back

Once he knocks off the chips
He picks up the large bowl
Which he dumps on his
12-year-old brother, poor soul!

It's the ultimate hit
Since the chips have now spread
On his shoulders and neck
On his chest and his head

As the 12-year-old plans
An attack, one that's great
His mom steps in between them
Before it's too late

She informs her two boys
They are grounded today
Plus, the 12-year-old
Must clean the mess right away

'That's not fair!', cries the 12-year-old
'He should clean, too!'
But his mom says
'You're older so this is on you!'

The boy yells, 'I must clean
Just because I am older?'
He looks annoyed
With that chip on his shoulder [1]

# JET FIASCO

As the pilot positions her jet plane to land
Something terrible happens, completely unplanned

Sparks fly out from the wheels as the jet scrapes the ground
These sparks turn into flames that spread quickly around

Once the jet has stopped moving, the pilot jumps out
Both in shock and hysterical, she then does shout

'I need help! I need help! Someone please save my jet!'
With the fire close by she is dripping with sweat

Even worse her jet's parked right beside a small plane
Which is also in flames that look tough to contain

Soon an airport attendant appears (his name's Will)
He can't calm down the pilot. She's freaking out still.

'I am dying! I'm dying because of this flame!
My life's ruined! It never will feel quite the same!'

The attendant is calm as he hands her a hose
(It shoots hundreds of gallons of water he knows)

The crazed pilot sprays water. It shoots everywhere.
It sprays onto the jet planes above in the air

But because this poor pilot is still full of nerves
When she aims the hose right at the flames the hose swerves

The attendant insists she calms down as she frets
'Everything will be fine after you cool your jets' [1]

# ZANY WORD BLENDER #2
## (vegetables)

If you spin a chimp twice near a snail     _____

It may gripe a bit, then start to wail     _____

Will the doc or nurse know     _____

Why a monkey's sick?  No!     _____

Hide the scar rotting under its tail     _____

*Inside each line, I hid **one** word*
*Combine them since, right now, they're blurred*

# BRAVE

Every school day at lunch
I sit down with a bunch
Of the popular kids in my school
Here sit Kaitlyn and Aiden
Brianna and Jayden
Each kid at this table is cool

Late last week Aiden bragged
About something he grabbed
After taking a swim in the lake
It was there on the land
Aiden grabbed with bare hand
A potentially venomous snake

Kaitlyn next told a story
Of her recent glory
When she flew above by trapeze
No, she never once fell
Yes, of course, she did well!
She trapezed with no hands, just her knees

These two kids sounded brave
From the stories they gave
Every kid was excited to hear
They snagged snakes with hands bare
And trapezed through the air
It was obvious they had no fear

It was my turn to gloat
But as I cleared my throat
I did not have a tale to impress
For I'd done nothing bold
If the truth had been told
And the pressure was causing me stress

Fearing some kids would scoff
I let out a fake cough
(It's a time-tested, sneaky old trick)
Then I stood up to go
Of course, I got up slow
(After all, I was suddenly sick)

As I threw out my food
In a terrible mood
Since my chance to impress had been blown
I approached this boy Tony
Who ate macaroni
And did so while sitting alone

Tony often got teased
Making teachers displeased
'Cool kids' told him to sit far away
Though I knew this was wrong
Sometimes I went along
For, if not, teasing might come my way

And then out of the blue
My heart knew what to do
I asked Tony if I could sit down
Quickly Tony said, 'Yes!'
(As I'm sure you could guess)
Soon a smile replaced his huge frown

Though I still wasn't able
To brag at that table
Or weave a tall tale sounding grave
I was bursting inside
With my new sense of pride
Knowing I had just done something brave

# STRAW-MAKING MILL

They make all types of straws in this straw-making mill
Here the straws are built well, so the drinks never spill

Once the straws have been built, they are sent down a line
The conveyor belt's new. On most days it works fine.

On this belt are two knobs. One reads *Slow*. One reads *Fast*.
Just above is one more. It reads *Powerful Blast*.

At the end of the belt, Grayson Wilkerson stands
He puts straws into boxes, does so with bare hands

When the belt is on *Slow*, Grayson grabs the straws well
But the pace is so slow he gets bored. You can tell.

When the belt is on *Fast*, Grayson grabs the straws, too
But because it's so fast, sometimes he'll miss a few

At the start of the day, the belt starts off on *Slow*
Grayson boxes 200 straws all in a row

Feeling bored after lunch, Grayson tries to push *Fast*
Accidentally, the boy pushes *Powerful Blast*

And the moment he does, the belt rattles about
Before hundreds of straws begin firing out

Straws fly off of the belt, on the floor, in the air
Some straws hit Grayson's head.  One straw lands in his hair.

Though he desperately reaches, it's to no avail
The straws slip through his fingers.  Poor Grayson does fail.

There's not much he can do.  Grayson's now a lost cause.
The belt's moving too fast so he's grasping at straws [I]

# MISTY BAKERSON

At the age of 16, Misty started dating Earl
Soon Earl fell in love with her.  She was a special girl.

Earl was quite romantic.  Quite a lady's man!  Such charm!
One day he surprised her with a tattoo on his arm

It read Misty Bakerson.  He showed it off with pride.
All his friends knew Earl was hoping she'd become his bride

After dinner, late one night, Earl dropped down on one knee
With a ring in hand he asked, 'Will you please marry me?'

Misty was completely shocked.  Her eyes soon filled with tears.
She said, 'No.  I'm way too young!  Check back in seven years.'

Earl was absolutely stunned.  He stood there in a daze.
Out of anger he yelled out, 'Let's go our separate ways!'

Earl refused to date for years.  His Misty wound still hurt.
Once his wound completely healed, Earl did begin to flirt

Soon Earl met his next true love, a stunning girl named Christie
When she saw Earl's arm tattoo, she asked, 'So who's this Misty?'

Earl tried changing topics, so embarrassed by his past
Now, with Christie in his life, his tattoo couldn't last

Earl searched 'round the Internet.  He typed tattoo removal.
If Earl could remove it he would have Christie's approval

Working on Earl's arm, the tattoo guy heard halfway through
'Please stop now!  This hurts too much!  I'll never make it through!'

Once he stopped and Earl looked down, his hands began to shake
Part of Earl's tattoo was gone, still left was his *Mist ake*

# POOR CHICKIE

After months of rehearsing
Tonight's the debut
All the chickens are ready
To see this thing through

They've been working for months
To remember their lines
Even if they forget
The director has signs

Chickie's super excited
To star in the show
She looks confident now
Chickie's ready to go!

As she exits her coop
Chickie hears her mom shout
'Break a leg, Superstar!
Really let it all out!'

Feeling confident
Chickie heads straight to the theater
Once she arrives
Some reporters do greet her

'How does it feel
Being such a big star?'
'Do you think when you're done
Kids will know who you are?'

Chickie know she'll be famous
She nods her head *yes*
Unaware, in short time
She'll be feeling distress

She excuses herself
Then heads off to review
All her lines from the play
There are more than a few

Once the moment arrives
And the first scene begins
She forgets all her lines
She just nervously grins

When it's her turn to speak
Chickie says not one word
No one knows what to do
This is truly absurd!

When a cast member whispers
'Do something and quick!'
Chickie whispers right back
'I feel terribly sick!'

Soon her stomach lets out
A large grumbling sound
Seconds later an egg
Tumbles onto the ground

As she bursts into tears
Chickie's fully aware
She is frozen on stage
This is such a nightmare!

Though her mom wished her luck
When she said, 'Break a leg!'
Chickie had the worst luck
Since she laid a big egg [1]

# CALENDAR MAKERS

Seven calendar makers use flawless technique
Each is tasked with creating one day of the week

Measured Mira gets Mondays (she's had them for years)
Tidy Tristan takes Tuesdays (his work never smears)

Willing Wyatt does Wednesdays (he likes those the best)
Thoughtful Theo has Thursdays (he draws them with zest)

Flawless Phoebe makes Fridays (they're fun she does say)
Selfless Skyler owns Saturdays (such a great day!)

Sadly, Sophie lands Sundays.  That day is the worst!
(She was hoping for Fridays, which Phoebe took first)

Every child produces one page every day
The block letters and pictures make quite a display

But this morning poor Mira is out 'cause she's sick
And her boss needs a Monday from somebody quick

Tristan raises his hand, says he'll make Mondays too.
His boss thanks him but warns, 'Two days are tough to do'

Tristan shrugs off the warning, prepares to amaze
In a couple of hours he's drafted both days

Tristan's boss checks his work then her whole body shakes
Disappointed she tells him about his mistakes

'You misspelled the word Monday.  There isn't a u.
And you also botched Tuesday, a word that you knew'

Tristan lowers his head knowing he messed up twice
Then he turns to his boss who provides some advice

'Please don't stress over this or you'll fail,' she does chime
'From now on simply take things one day at a time' [1]

# ZANY WORD BLENDER #3
## (soccer)

If this class is too hard you will fail      _____

Trust me, that wouldn't be a fine tale      _____

Long ago Alex tried      _____

He admits now he cried      _____

So much grief if a boy has to wail      _____

*Inside each line, I hid **one** word*
*Combine them since, right now, they're blurred*

# CHRISTMAS TREE FOR SALE

In this Christmas tree shop, they sell nothing but trees
There are pines, there are firs, and whatever you please

These tall trees, full of needles, are healthy and clean
Which the shoppers expect from a true evergreen

Not too far from these trees, a small bush lies about
It is shriveled and dying with leaves falling out

Not surprising, this bush lies here day after day
As the beautiful evergreens get swept away

To spur interest the store owner tries to entice
The tree shoppers to buy the poor bush, 'It's half-price!'

And it works, just a little, one boy sees the sign
Then compares the small bush to an eight-foot-tall pine

Still aware the cheap price won't alone be enough
The store owner then offers the boy other stuff

'If you buy this bush now, you'll get free tinsel too.
Plus a stocking and wreath, all these gifts are for you'

The boy's very impressed.  He considers the deal.
But he doesn't commit (the bush has no appeal)

Now the owner who's desperate to sell it today
Drops the price of the bush (will she give it away?)

The boy ponders her offer.  It's practically free!
Though it's cheap does he want such a lame Christmas tree?

As the owner attempts to make one final push
The boy wavers once more.  He still beats 'round the bush. [1]

# EMPTY BEACHES

They've closed every beach in the great state of Maine
So, of course, the whole summer the children complain

In New Hampshire they've gone and shut down Hampton Beach
'It's off limits!', the mayor declares in a speech

What about Massachusetts?  They've blocked off Cape Cod.
It's completely deserted.  This looks a bit odd.

In New Jersey they've quarantined all of the shore
And Long Island, New York is abandoned.  What for?

They have blocked off Virginia, all summer they say
Same with Georgia and Florida, they're empty today

With no people around, no one ever gets hurt
No one gets sunburned badly not wearing a shirt

No one worries the sun block will get in their eyes
No one trips over waves, ends up injured or cries

All these beaches are safe since there's nobody here
Now's the best time to go since the (East) coast is clear [1]

# UTENSIL DROPPING

The *Utensil Drop* game is about to begin
The contestants today are Samantha and Finn

Each kid picks a utensil: a fork or a spoon
Which they'll drop in a bucket sometime around noon

In this bucket are one-dollar bills. There are eight.
These bills float on the water awaiting their fate

If a kid's fork or spoon touches even one bill
Then they're out of the game. Yes, this game involves skill!

What's the prize if one wins? He or she keeps the cash.
That's eight dollars one earns, just like that, in a flash!

As Samantha and Finn map their strategies out
The utensils they'll choose look quite different, no doubt

The spoon's bowl is too wide and its handle too tall
The fork's tines are so narrow. Its handle so small.

Seeing two different sizes, Samantha replies
'I am taking the fork!' (This is not a surprise.)

As Finn picks up the spoon and looks 10 feet below
The large bucket awaits him. It's his turn to go.

Finn plans nothing at all. He just drops his spoon in.
The spoon hits not one bill. Finn is likely to win!

Though Samantha was pretty convinced Finn would lose
She feels confident since the thin fork she did choose

As she studies the bills, tracking every small move
She lines up her thin fork. She has something to prove.

As Samantha's fork falls, it is lined up quite well
It's unlikely to touch any bill, she can tell

Just before her forks lands, and as if by command
Four bills cluster beneath where her fork's gonna land

The fork's tines pierce the bills halfway through (maybe more)
Poor Samantha has lost. She thought she'd win, for sure.

Though Finn tries not to laugh (after all, this is funny)
He states quite bluntly, 'Fork over the money' [1]

# ART GALLERY

Around 7:15, this past Saturday night
The art gallery boss shouted, 'Something's not right!'

All the paintings were taken down off of the wall
All the nails were removed.  There were none left at all.

And where there were once holes, there was plaster and paint
When the boss saw this wall, my, she nearly did faint!

For the art gallery was approaching and soon
It was scheduled to open on Sunday at noon

With no workers around to assist the poor boss
Knowing she'd have to work the whole night she felt cross

For the next 16 hours, the boss worked straight through
She put 500 nails in the wall.  This is true!

She hung all of the paintings (200 or more)
It was now Sunday morning (near noon, just before)

With an eager crowd waiting outside to come in
The boss thought she had made it and let out a grin

The grin turned to a frown when she saw on the floor
A large pile of nails right beside the main door

With just three seconds left and still sporting that frown
The boss shoved all the nails in her mouth and bit down

Then the boss closed her lips so nobody could see
All the nails she was biting in her gallery

As the patrons walked in, her mood turned a bit brighter
She made it barely.  It was a nail-biter. [1]

# SCIENTIST JEB

A long time ago, long before you were born
A mad scientist lived, he was named Jeb McZorn

Jeb did crazy experiments all on his own
Most took place in his basement when Jeb was alone

On one cold winter night, a small spider appeared
This gave Jeb an idea. One that was a tad weird.

He kept feeding it spinach, for months, all day long
'By the time we are done you will feel mighty strong!'

It turned out Jeb was right. Soon this spider once meek
Bulged with muscles all over in less than a week!

After weaving small webs that too often would fall
Now Jeb's spider weaved ones that were 90 feet tall

They were not only tall, they were sturdy webs, too
Jeb declared, 'Let's go see what your new strength can do'

'We shall travel the world. We'll leave later today!'
And they did. By that night, they arrived in Bombay.

There a very large web his strong spider first spun
'Keep on spinning your web. We have only begun!'

Soon the spider extended its web to Japan
Next it weaved that same web all the way to Iran

The strong spider kept spinning its web in Bahrain
It weaved all around Turkey and Belgium and Spain

Not long after Jeb's spider spun into Peru
The web stretched to Brazil and to Mexico, too

At last Jeb and his spider arrived in L.A.
Where they finished the web later on that same day

'We have spun a great web everywhere around Earth
'My experiment worked for whatever that's worth!'

They completed this web 35 years ago
Yet this fact is one very few children do know

So when you go online, and you're searching the 'net
It's important this fact you don't ever forget

Please remember that it was mad scientist Jeb
Whose strong spider created the first World Wide Web [P]

# Brett's Bio

Brett Fleishman grew up in the suburbs of Philadelphia. In 1995, he earned his B.A. In 2001, he earned his M.B.A. At no point did he earn a roster spot in the N.B.A. Since 2001, Brett has been living with his two sons, Jacob and Dylan, in the greater Boston area. (Please note that, while Brett and his sons enjoy living in Boston, their sports allegiances remain firmly Philadelphian.)

To learn more about Brett, please check out his bio at **www.brettfleishman.com**. You can also follow him on Facebook (Funny Bone Tickling Poetry) and on Instagram (@funnyboneticklingpoetry).

# Also by Brett Fleishman

**If the Earth is Round...** is a compilation of 21 funny-bone-tickling poems designed for beginner readers and for adults who love reading to young children.

**Twist and Shout!** is a compilation of 33 funny-bone-tickling poems designed for intermediate readers.
Please be aware...this book is extremely punny!

# APPENDIX

# WORDPLAYS

I love to include wordplays in my poems, especially at the very end of the poems. My favorite wordplays are puns and idioms, but there are other types of wordplays, too. In case you don't know (or forget!) what puns and idioms are, here's a quick overview.

# HOMONYMS

Wait, what? I just said we were going to review puns and idioms. Now, I'm also adding in homonyms? Not cool. I know. Not cool at all.

In order to understand what a pun is, you have to first understand what a homonym is.

A homonym is a word that is spelled one way, but has more than one meaning.

*Bright* is a homonym because it means either of the following:

1.      Full of light
2.      Intelligent

# PUNS

OK, so why did I make you learn about homonyms before learning about puns?

Because a pun is simply a joke that makes use of more than one meaning of a homonym.

Let's stick with the previous example. When Thomas Edison invented the light bulb, someone could have said, jokingly, 'Now, THAT was a pretty bright idea!' Would that person have been referring to how intelligent Thomas Edison must have been to come up with a new invention? Maybe. Would that person have been referring to the brightness of the actual light bulb? Maybe. Either definition works. And that's what makes puns punny. I mean, funny.

# IDIOMS

An idiom is a phrase that makes absolutely no sense when the words are read *literally* (exactly as described).

*It's raining cats and dogs* is an idiom because cats and dogs don't actually fall out of the sky when it rains. (At least not where I live, they don't.)

Yet, somehow, people realize that these nonsensical phrases have a totally different meaning. When people recognize that a nonsensical phrase has a different meaning, it means they understand the phrase *figuratively*.

Let's go back to the idiom *it's raining cats and dogs*. People recognize (somehow) that this phrase simply means, *figuratively*, that it's raining really, really hard.

I frequently include idioms at the end of my poems. What makes them funny (well, to me, at least!) is that they not only work *figuratively*, but also *literally*.

..........

Is your brain hurting yet? Yeah, my brain hurts, too. Enough with the boring definitions...

What follows are explanations for all of the wordplays in this book.

# POEMS WITH PUNS

## CHECK, PRETTY PLEASE?

The term *check mate* refers to a situation in chess when one player announces that he or she has captured the opponent's king. In this poem, I use the term differently. After leaving several subtle hints that the restaurant is closing soon, the waiter decides it is time to confront the kings more directly. Though some customers think it is rude if the waiter or waitress leaves the check before they ask for it (since some customers feel like they are being rushed), this waiter runs out of patience when he tells them, 'I'll get your check mates.' Of course, the customers are kings so *check mates* is a subtle reference to the chess meaning, too.

## TUG-OF-WAR

Most times when you hear the term well done, it is used to let someone know that he or she has done a good job. In this poem, Captain Steak is proud of his team for winning the Tug-of-War contest, so it makes sense that he would congratulate them for a job well done. The term *well done* also describes the temperature of a steak. More specifically, *well done* in this context means the steak is cooked fully. Since the steaks were playing Tug-of-War over piping hot coals, it is quite likely that they were fully cooked (or *well done*) by the time the game ended.

## SCIENTIST JEB

This is one of my Mom's favorite poems. For the millennials out there, the *World Wide Web* is a dated term that refers to the Internet. The first letters of the words *World Wide Web* are *www*. Check out pretty much any website address, and you will notice the address begins with these three letters. In this poem, Scientist Jeb's spider becomes the first spider to weave a web all around the world. Therefore, the spider has created the first *World Wide Web*. I mention in the poem that this event happened 35 years ago, which is around the same time when the Internet became more mainstream. I'm not saying you should thank Scientist Jeb's spider for Instagram, but... perhaps you should?

# POEMS WITH IDIOMS

## WEIGHTLIFTING CONTEST

If you *raise the bar* it means you do something that exceeds expectations. In this poem, each weightlifter takes turns trying to prove he is stronger than the other. Since each lift is more challenging than the last, the weightlifters keep *raising the bar* (trying to exceed expectations). Of course, on the final lift, the weightlifter actually raises the bar, so this idiom works literally and figuratively.

## SCHOOL BUS FACTORY TOUR

If you *throw someone under the bus* it means you blame someone else when something goes wrong. In this poem, Russ's boss is embarrassed when his tour group sees the oil spill on the floor next to the new school bus. Rather than accept the blame for this leak, the boss gets angry and ultimately blames Russ instead. Worse yet, the boss loses his temper and shoves Russ who falls down and lands under the actual school bus. Therefore, this idiom works both figuratively (since the boss blames Russ for the oil spill) and literally (since the boss actually shoves Russ who lands under the school bus).

## STOP SIGN FIASCO

If you *pull out all the stops*, it means you do everything possible to be successful. In this poem, the cops agree to pull out all 35 stop signs by the end of the day. Though the cops work as hard as they can, it looks like they are not going to accomplish this ambitious goal. Somehow, through hard work and tireless effort, they ultimately (just barely) succeed. Since the cops did everything within their power to accomplish their goal, they figuratively *pulled out all the stops*. Of course, since their goal was to actually pull out all 35 stop signs, they also literally pulled out all the stops.

# POEMS WITH IDIOMS

## RODEO RICK

If you are *back in the saddle*, it means you are doing something that you haven't done in a very long time. After not riding a horse for many years, Rodeo Rick finally agrees (thanks to Val's convincing!) to ride a horse again. So, figuratively, Rodeo Rick is *back in the saddle* again since he is doing something that he hasn't done for years. Since what he hasn't done for years is ride a horse, and since you sit on a saddle when you ride a horse, Rodeo Rick is also literally back in the saddle again.

## LOTTERY TICKET

The idioms *down the drain* means wasted or lost. In this poem, Jay purchases a lottery ticket and hopes to win the $12 million jackpot. Not surprisingly, Jay is excited from the outset and even more excited as the T.V. announcer reads off numbers that match the numbers on Jay's ticket. Suffice it to say, Jay's hopes of winning the jackpot get higher and higher with each matching number. Shortly before hearing the sixth and final number, Jay accidentally knocks the ticket into the sink. While desperately trying to save the ticket, Jay hears he did, in fact, win the lottery. Yet, sadly, Jay is unable to save the ticket which literally goes down the drain of the kitchen sink. Of course, Jay's hopes have also figuratively gone *down the drain*.

## POTATO CHIP WAR

If you have *a chip on your shoulder*, it means you are holding a grudge against someone (and likely annoyed at that person). In this poem, the mom insists that the 12-year-old boy clean up the potato chip mess that he and his six-year-old brother made. His mom's point is that he should have known better because he is older. The 12-year-old boy disagrees. Both boys made the mess. Why should *he* have to clean it up by himself? Since the 12-year-old boy is annoyed at his mom (and likely to hold a grudge against her) for making him clean up the mess by himself, he figuratively is carrying a *chip on his shoulder*. Of course, since this dispute occurs shortly after the potato chip fight, the 12-year-old boy also literally has a chip on his shoulder.

# POEMS WITH IDIOMS

### JET FIASCO

If someone tells you to *cool your jets*, they are basically telling you to calm down. In this poem, the pilot (understandably) starts freaking out when she notices her jet plane is on fire. She is so anxious about what's happening that she is unable to aim the hose at the flames to put the fire out. The attendant tells the pilot to *cool her jets* because, figuratively, she needs to calm down in order to put the fire out. If, for some reason, she is able to calm down, then the pilot will be able to aim the hose at the flames and, literally, cool her jet plane.

### STRAW-MAKING MILL

If you are *grasping at straws*, it means you are making a desperate attempt to accomplish or figure out something. In this poem, Grayson helps out with the straw production process, gathering the straws as they move down the conveyor belt. When Grayson accidentally hits *Powerful Blast*, the straws begin to move down the conveyor belt very quickly. So quickly, in fact, that Grayson is unable to grab all of them before they start shooting passed him. Though he tries his best, Grayson is unable to gather all of the straws, so he is figuratively *grasping at straws*. Since his actual job is to grab the straws, Grayson is also literally grasping at straws.

### POOR CHICKIE

If you *lay an egg*, it means you do something poorly in front of other people. In this poem, Chickie, the star of the show, is expecting to perform well on stage. When Chickie forgets all of her lines when the show begins, she figuratively *lays an egg*. As she freaks out, Chickie (who, of course, happens to be a chicken) accidentally lays an actual egg, so she lays an egg literally, too. Bonus points to those who recognized the other idiom in this poem...hopefully Chickie's Mom wasn't wishing for her daughter to literally break her leg!

# POEMS WITH IDIOMS

## CALENDAR MAKERS

If you *take things one day at a time*, it means you take care of things as they happen and don't worry about the future. In this poem, Tristan offers to make the word *Monday* for the calendar, something that his sick friend Mira usually does. Tristan, meanwhile, typically makes the word *Tuesday*. When he attempts to make both days at the same time, Tristan ends up making mistakes --- and ultimately feels badly about them. When Tristan's boss tells him not to worry about these mistakes, she is figuratively telling him to take things one day at a time. Of course, since Tristan was successful when he was responsible for one day (*Monday*) only, it is also reasonable to believe his boss was, literally, telling him to take things one day at a time.

## CHRISTMAS TREE FOR SALE

If you *beat around the bush*, it means you avoid answering a question or waste time. In this poem, a boy sees a small, wilting bush next to a bunch of tall, beautiful Christmas trees. Though the store owner entices the boy to buy the bush by offering him a discount, it's clear that the boy is hesitant to buy the bush. Since the boy struggles to make a decision, he is figuratively *beating around the bush*. Of course, what he's not making a decision about is buying the actual bush, so he is literally beating around (or, at the very least, standing around) the bush.

## EMPTY BEACHES

The idiom *the coast is clear* means it is safe to do something because no one is watching or preventing you from doing something. In this poem, all of the beaches on the East Coast of the United States are closed. There are no people at the beaches. If kids wanted to go to one of these beaches, they could probably do so since there is no one there to stop them. So, figuratively, *the coast is clear*. Of course, because no one is on any of the beaches along the East Coast of the United States, the coast is literally clear.

# POEMS WITH IDIOMS

## UTENSIL DROPPING

The idiom *fork over the money* refers to a situation where the first person tells the second person to give the first person money (when the second person really doesn't want to give the first person money). In this poem, Finn beats Samantha in a utensil-dropping game where each kid tries to drop a utensil into a bucket of water without touching the dollar bills that are floating in the bucket of water. When Samantha's fork hits the dollar bills (after Finn's spoon did not hit any of the dollar bills), she loses the game and owes Finn some money. Though she doesn't want to, Samantha has to figuratively *fork over the money*. Of course, since Samantha's fork just impaled four dollar bills, she also has to fork over the money literally.

## ART GALLERY

The idiom *nail biter* refers to a tense situation where the outcome of an event isn't known until the very last minute. Since the art gallery owner is desperately trying to clean up her art gallery before the first patrons arrive, and it's unclear whether she will be able to do so in time, her situation is figuratively a *nail biter*. When the art gallery owner sees a bunch of nails on her floor right before the patrons arrive, out of desperation she shoves all of the nails into her mouth so the gallery appears tidy. As she bites down on those nails, it is literally a nail biter.

# ANSWER KEY FOR ZANY WORD BLENDERS

### #1
*(boy names)*

Sam
Ryan
Pat
Sean
Dan

### #2
*(vegetables)*

spinach
pea
corn
yam
carrot

### #3
*(soccer)*

assist
net
goal
head
FIFA

CPSIA information can be obtained
at www.ICGtesting.com
Printed in the USA
FSOW03n0710141217
42074FS